PIONEER VALLEY EDUCATIONAL PRESS, INC

LIFE AT THE
BEACH

ROSE LEWIS

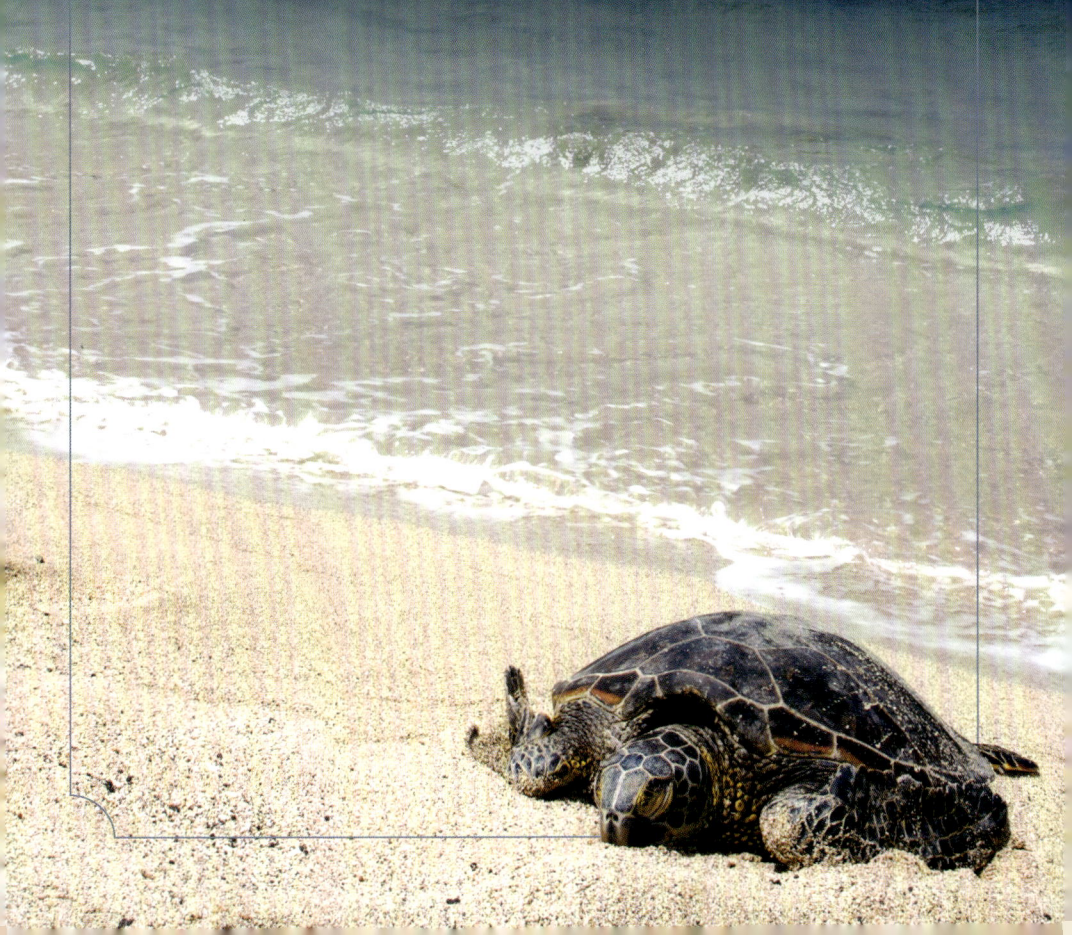

Look at the seagull.

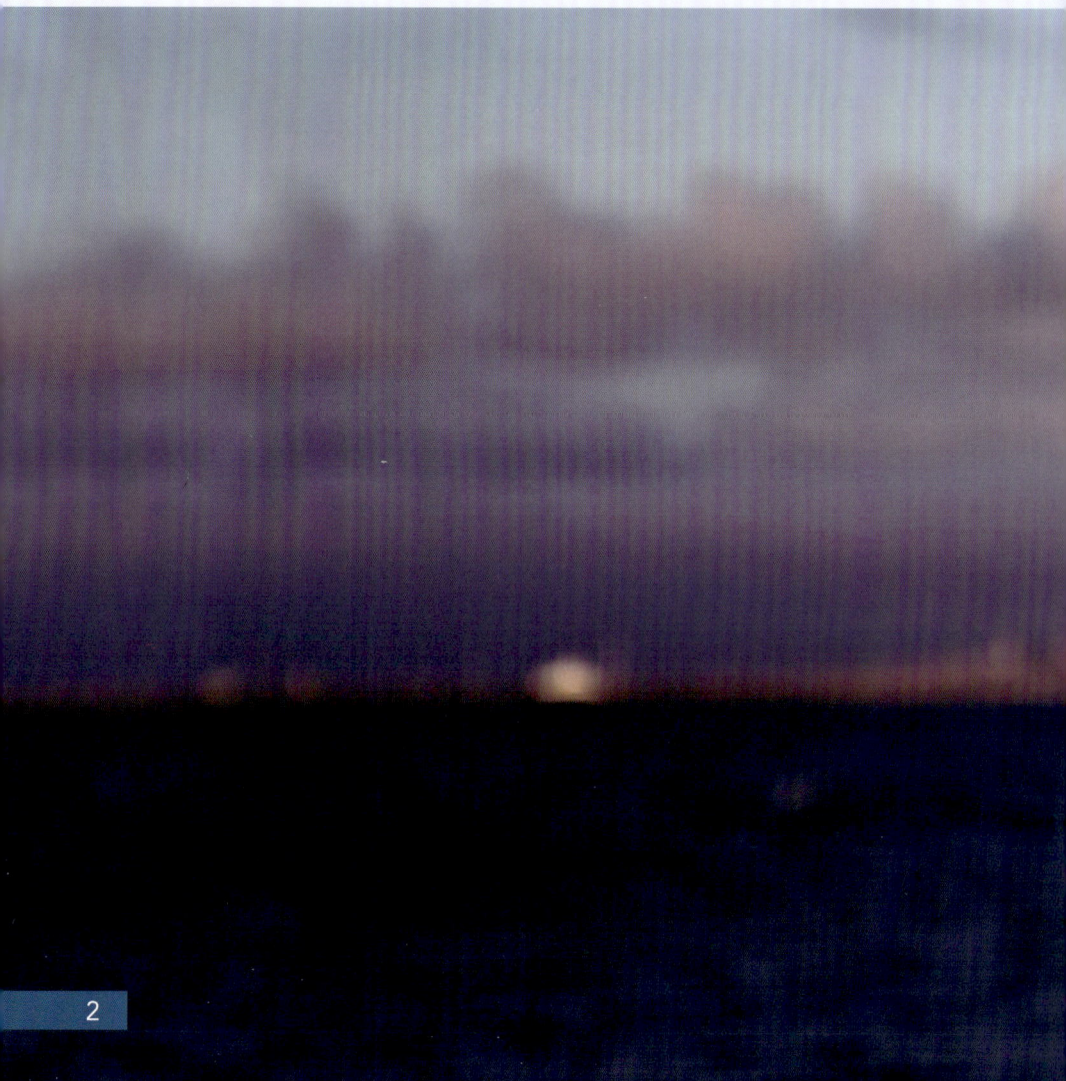

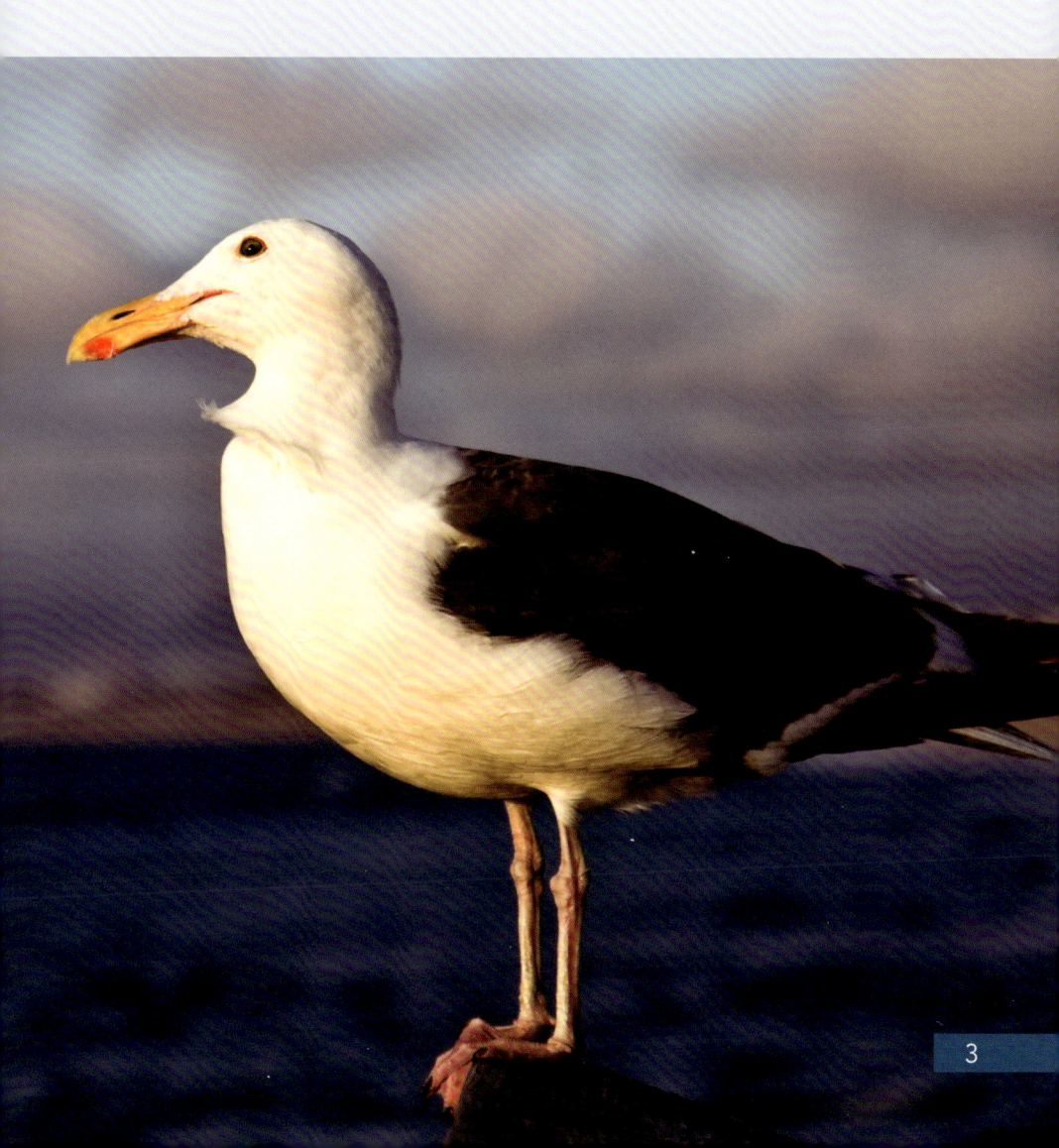

Look at the crab.

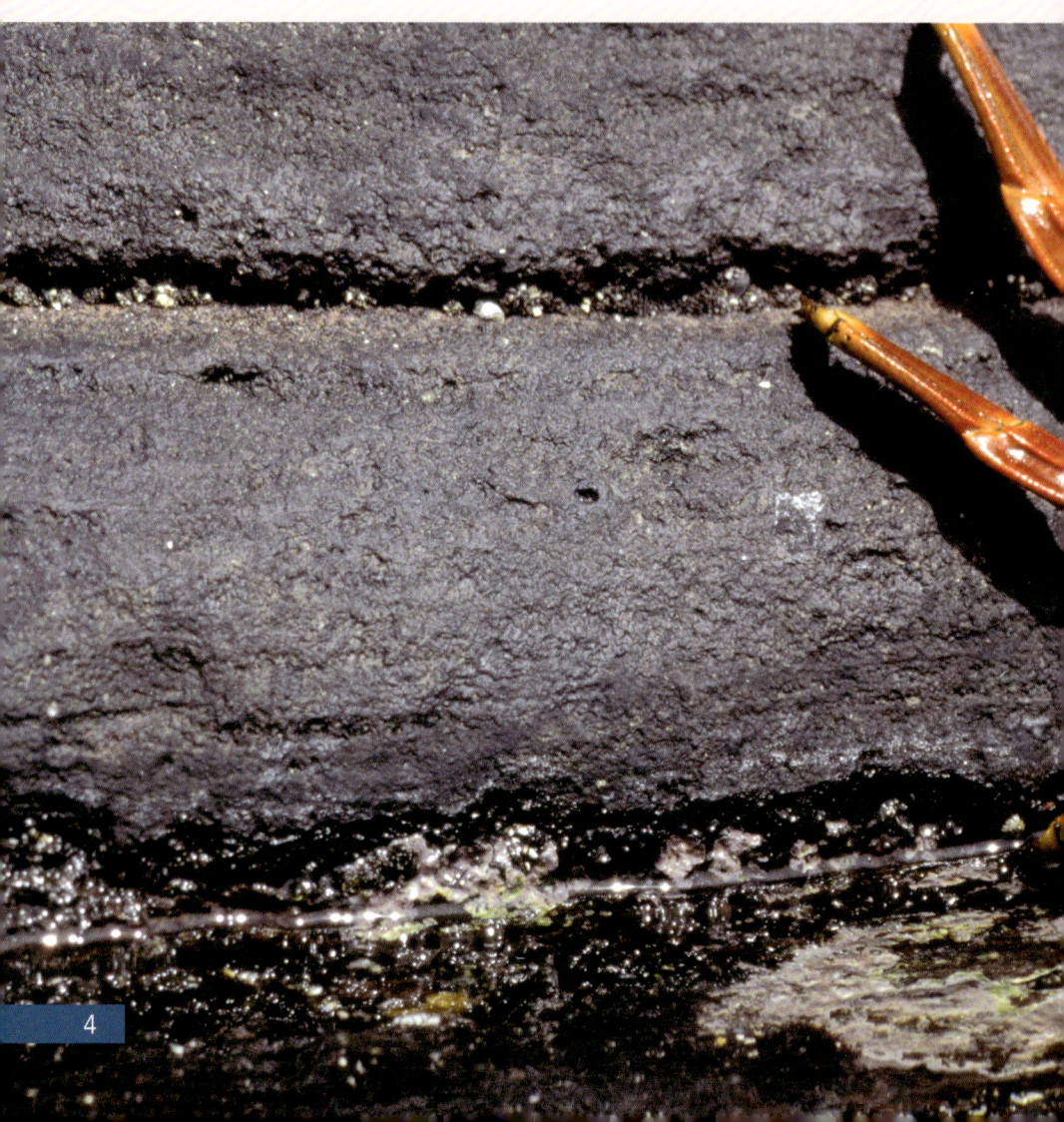

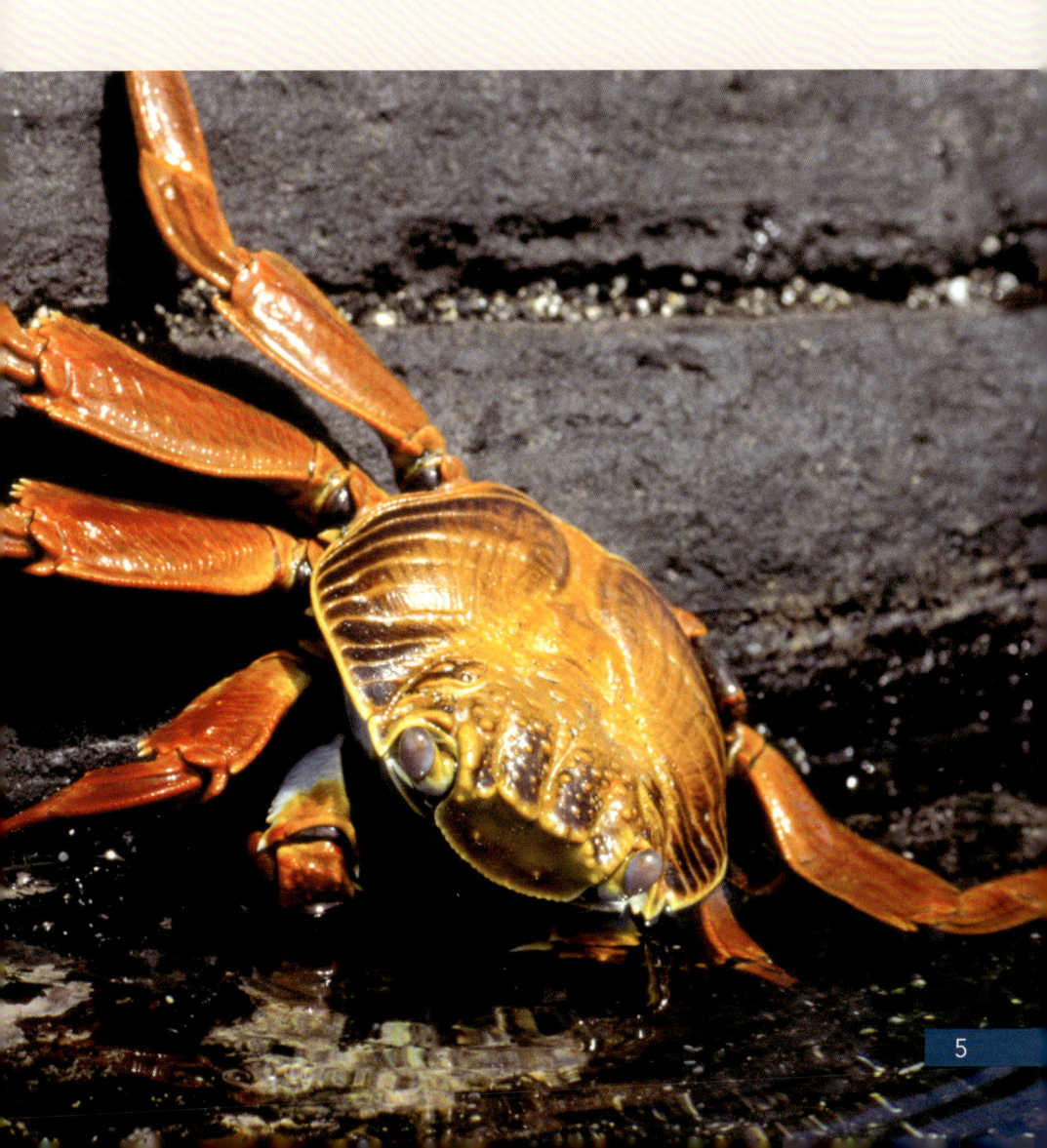

5

Look at the anemone.

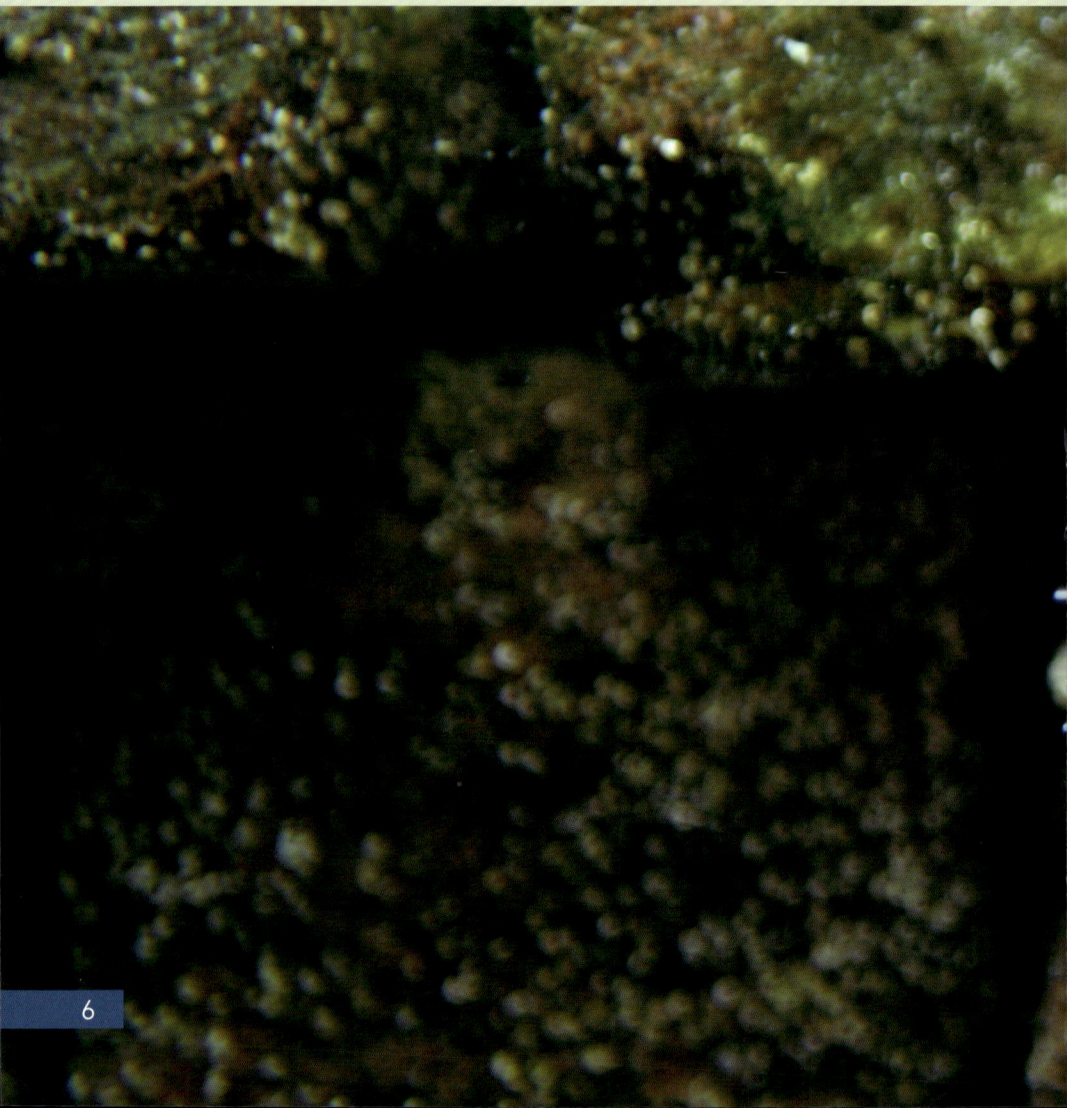

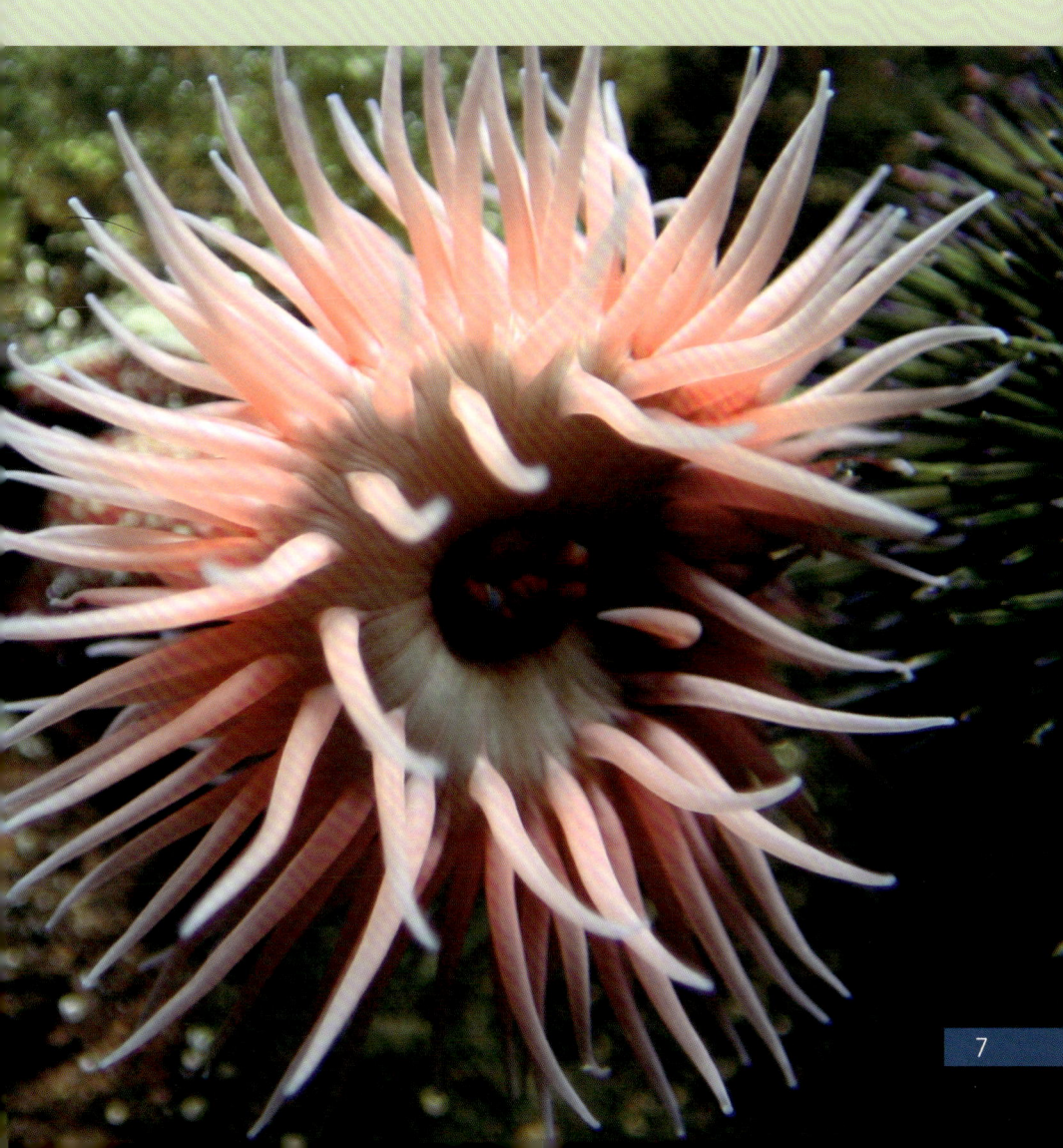

Look at the starfish.

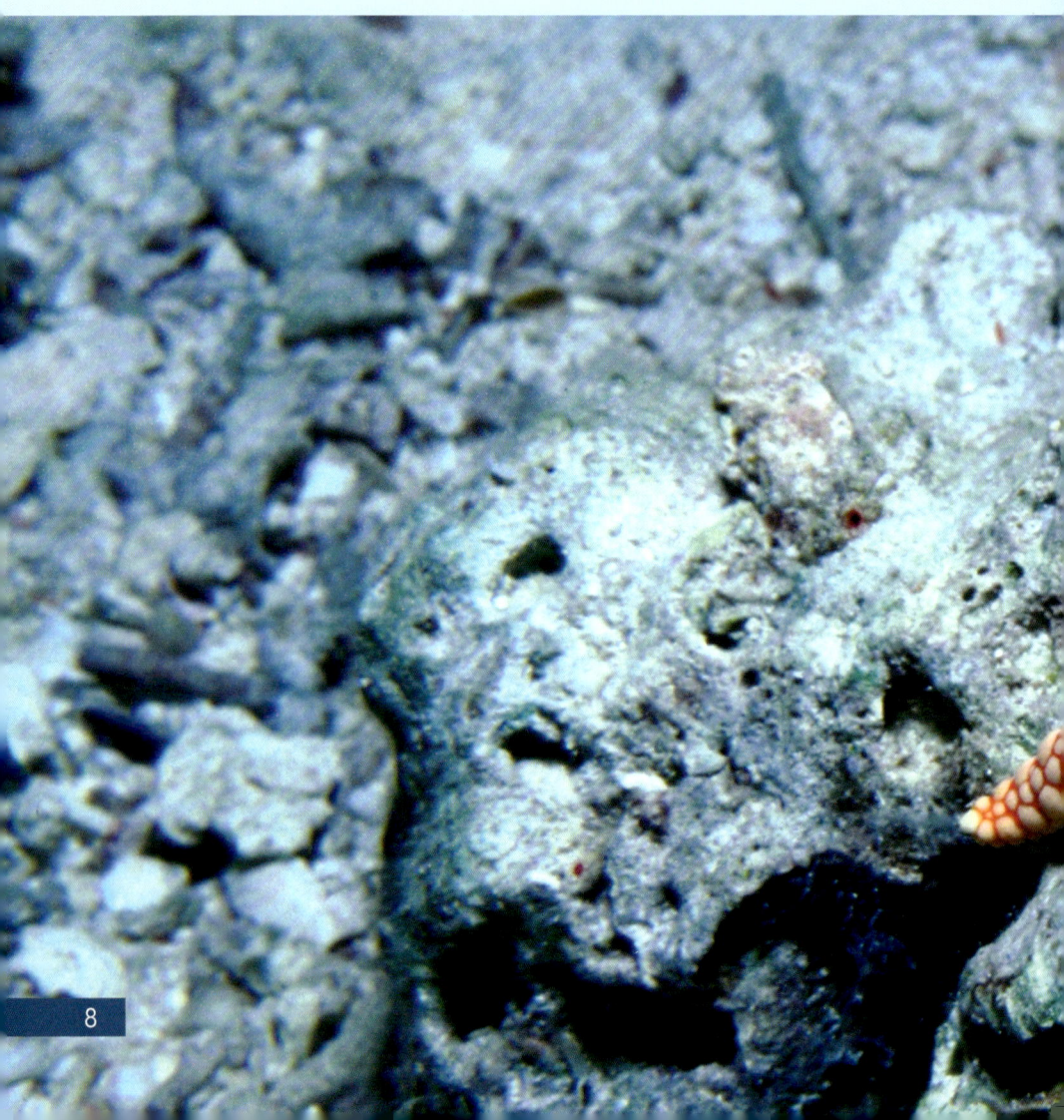

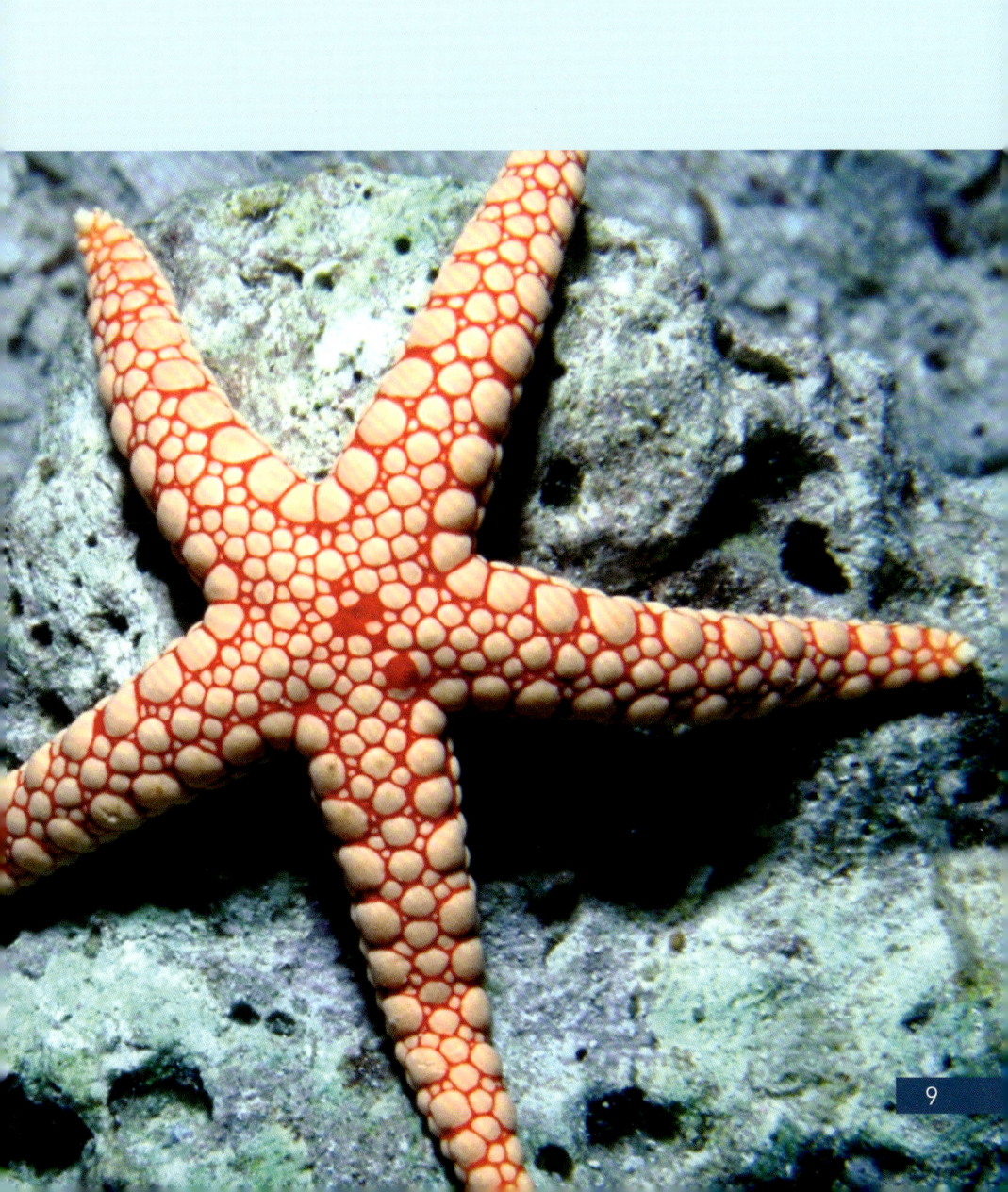

Look at the turtle.

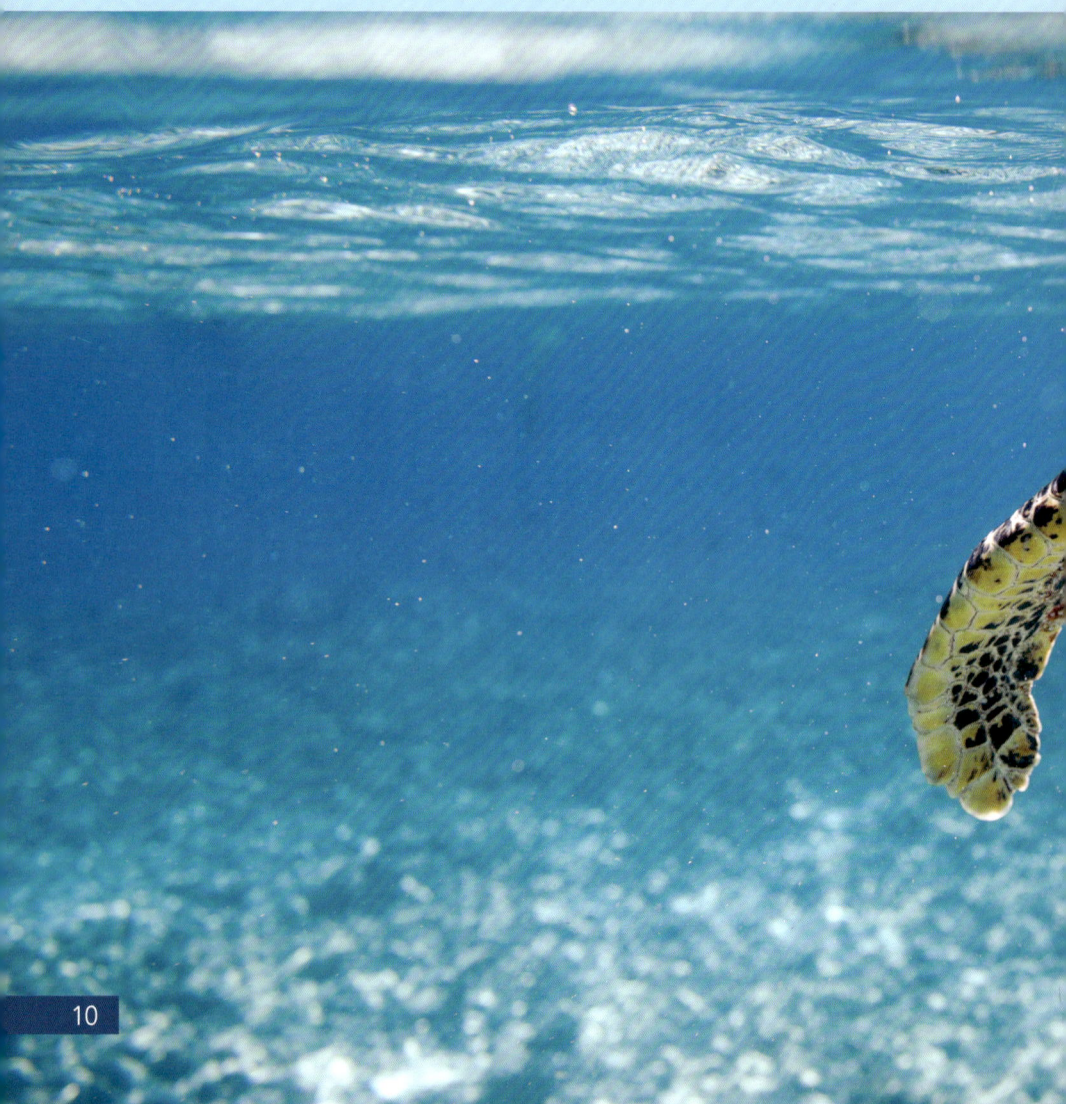

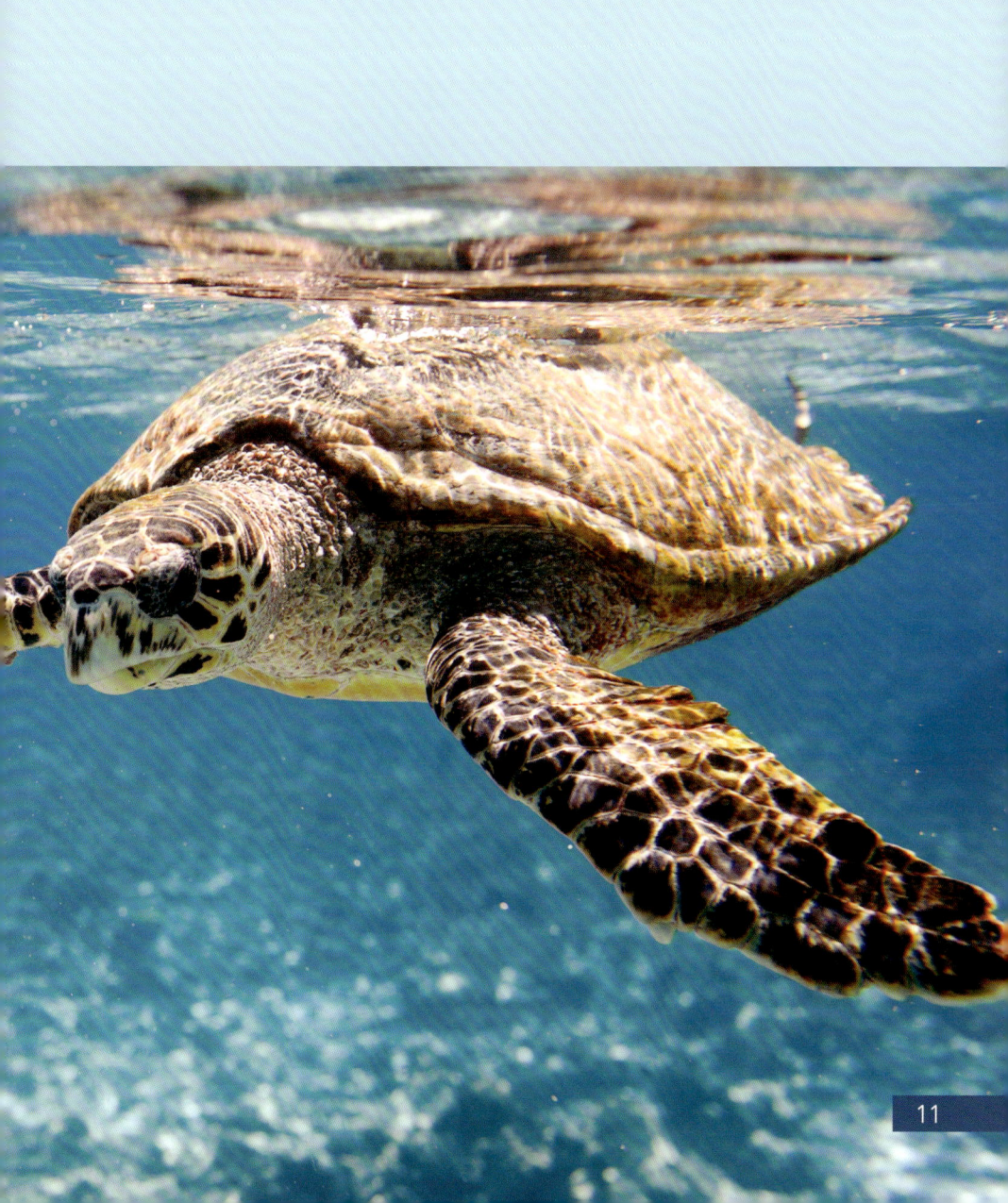

Look at the clam.

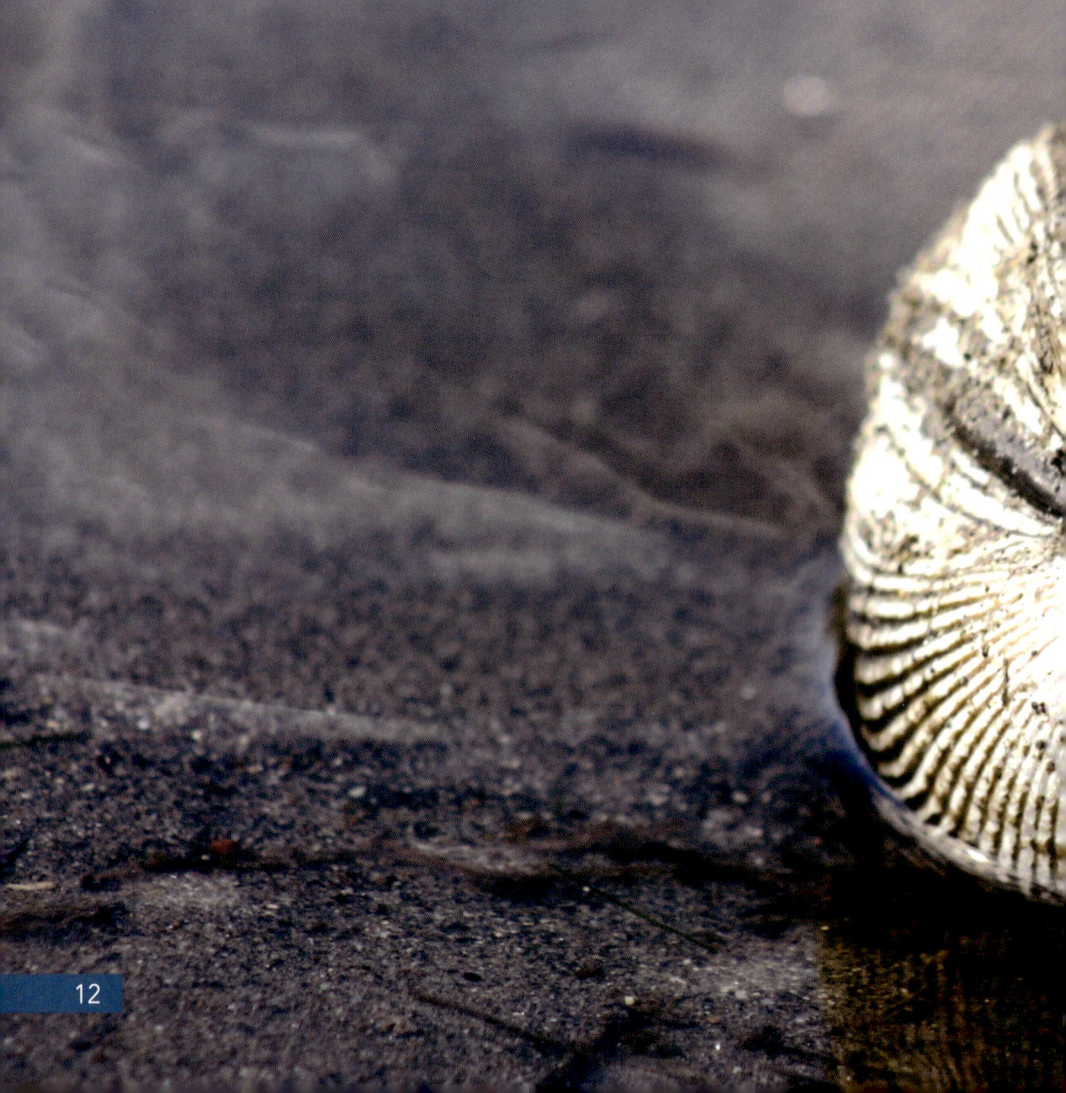

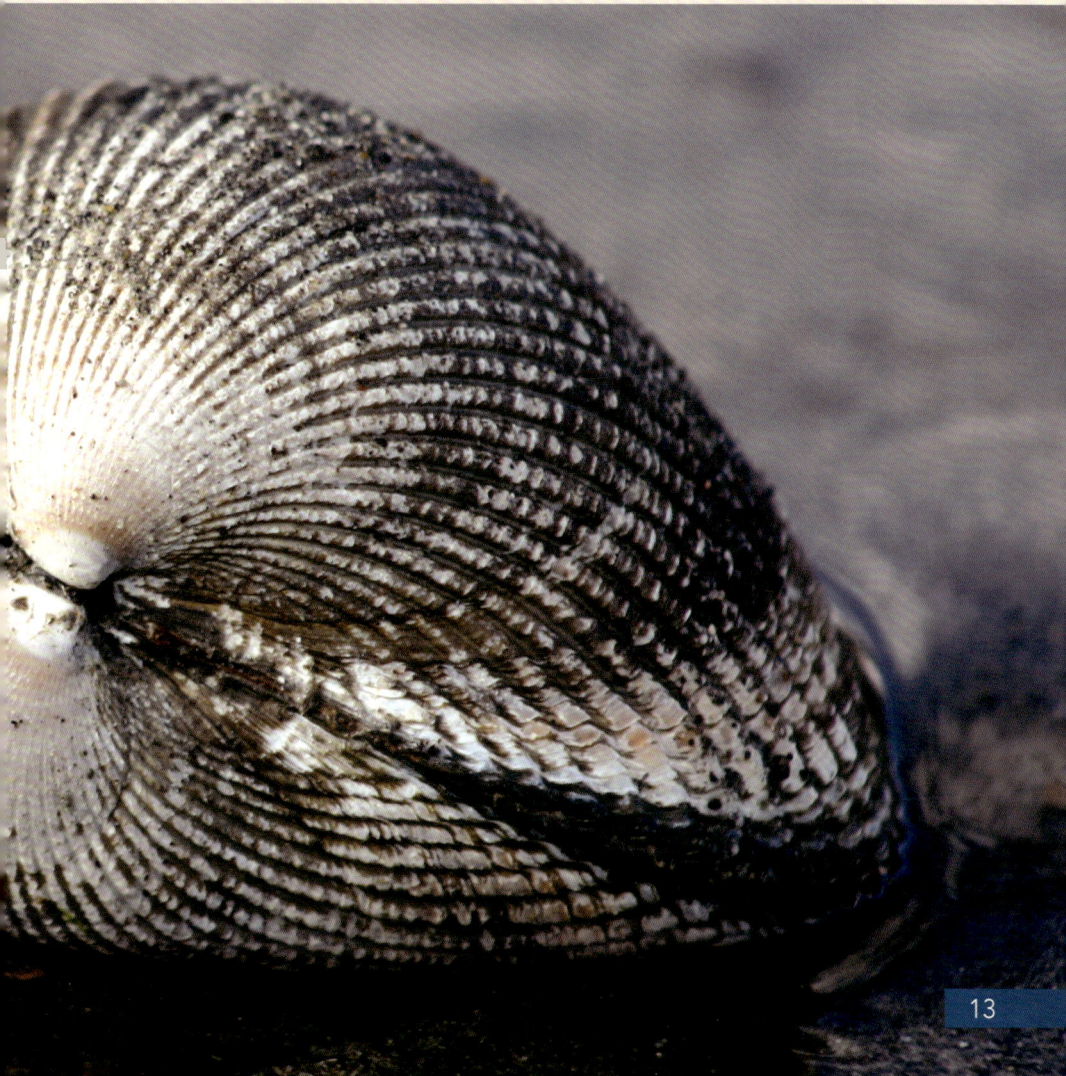

Look at the jellyfish.

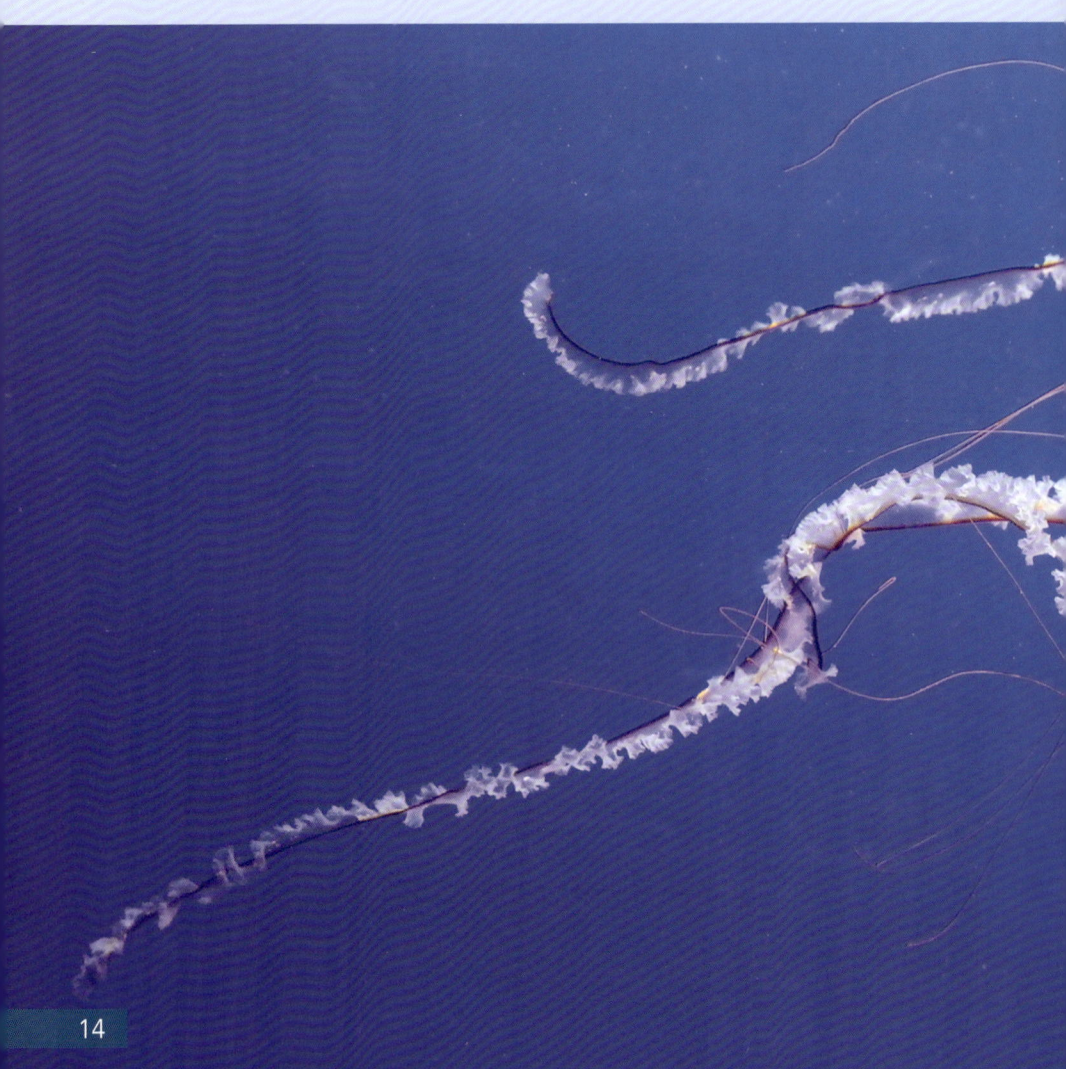

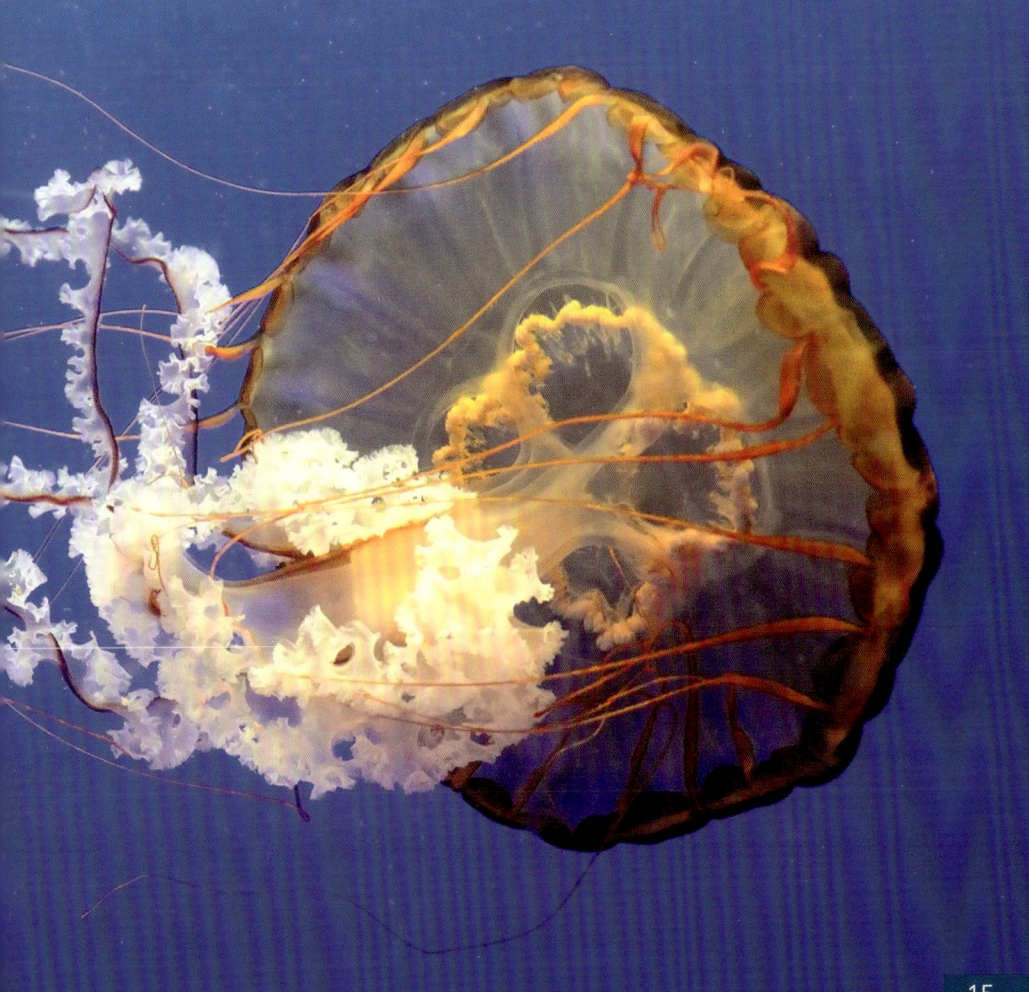

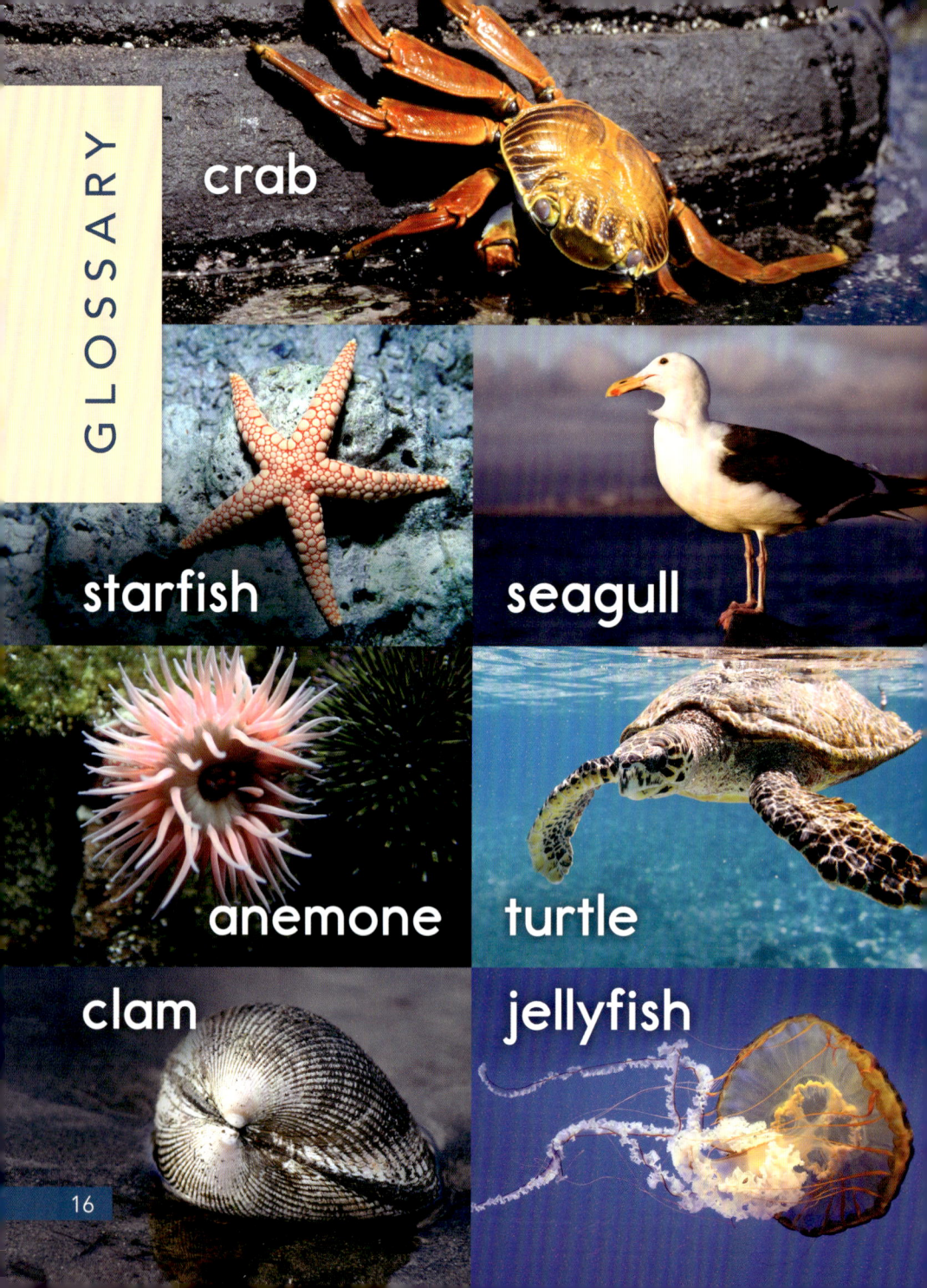